THE BOOK OF NO SELF

SCOTT MOSS

APOCRYPHILE
PRESS

APOCRYPHILE PRESS
PO Box 255
Hannacroix, NY 12087

Please join our mailing list at
www.apocryphilepress.com/free
We'll keep you up to date on all our new releases,
and we'll also invite you to download a FREE BOOK.
Visit us today!

INTRODUCTION

Dear reader,

This book is not poetry, although on the page it may look like it. One of the main inspirations for this work is the *Tao Te Ching*. Although I don't know Chinese, let alone ancient Chinese, I have imitated the brevity and verse format that appear in the best translations of this masterful work. The book itself is inspired by years of reading ancient and modern spiritual texts and listening to spiritual talks from around the world. It is an amalgamation of things that have seeped into "my" consciousness. I would not have written this book if there had not been significant glimpses of what the book speaks about.

As a cohesive whole, the book is designed to resist labels and categories because that is just the type of energy that prevents the dropping away of the illusion of twoness. Creating *Thisism* (the word *this* will be explained momentarily) or something similar would be oxymoronic. This does not depend upon hierarchy, authority, or institutional structure. Although even that doesn't make any sense. This is nothing.

There is no narrative at all to the work, so the order of the sections is somewhat arbitrary and unimportant, but it is nice to balance it out because some sections have certain modes that make sense to intersperse rather than pile up. So, in the words of Jean-Luc Godard regarding modern cinema, a film should have a beginning, a middle, and an end, but not necessarily in that order. I love that quote, and it applies to the free-flowing non-structure of the book.

Because this is a work that will be updated for as long as I read books, there will likely be a *Deathbed Edition*. If I don't die in a bed, there will be something like a *Hit while Jaywalking Edition* or a *Sniveling on a Sinking Ship Edition*.

If you are familiar with spiritual texts such as the *Tao Te Ching, The New Testament,* or the *Bhagavad Gita,* as well as many others, some of these passages may seem like echoes. None of these passages are "mine," and I don't mean that in the sense that I'm plagiarizing, although I certainly am lifting bits from the classics and elsewhere (I hope that the literary executors of *The Upanishads* don't come after me), but in the sense that there is no autonomous separate self that can possibly be in possession of anything at all.

When twoness reverts back to oneness, it is indescribably wonderful. The story of the self that most of us carry around all of our waking hours dissolves away and there is simply Being with a capital B. When it does reëmerge, it is similar to waking up but on a level that is categorically different, although the metaphor of waking up is possibly the best one. And yet there is something in all of us that remembers this. It feels like the joy of childhood.

The traditional Buddhist metaphor advises not to mistake a finger pointing at the moon for the moon itself. The more you focus on the finger, the less likely you will see the moon. Suffice to say that these words are pointing to something that transcends the words themselves. Don't let the words become orthodoxy, dogma, or something that the mind gets possession of to believe in.

Language has its limits, especially when talking about *this*, so reading the words presented here without seeing beyond the words themselves is constricting, as in the above metaphor. Language is also by its very nature dualistic, meaning it divides up the world into parts that interact with one another rather than all of existence and nonexistence being oneness. Some of these passages inevitably use dualistic language, implying that there is a separate self who can control things, but this language is somewhat inevitable.

The original short-run title of this volume was *This, On the Illusion of Self*. The word *this* has a meaning, or rather a non-meaning, that it's best to go over a bit. Similar to *Tao* in the best translations of the book *Tao Te Ching*, *this* can refer to love, eternity, harmony, god, spirit, and any number of other words. It is purposefully vague so as to be unnaildownable, as is a zen koan.

The word *you* is sometimes used to mean the illusion of the self, and sometimes it is simply the grammatical structure that is necessary to communicate. Both of these forms appear, but it should be rather obvious which is which by the context.

Terms used throughout such as liberation, enlightenment, oneness, God, etc., are different ways of referring to the same thing. No single word is used over and over so as to avoid the temptation of creating a religion around a single word or concept.

There is some playful language in this book that breaks conventions in an attempt to bypass reason and logic which tend to be oppressive. Paradox and nonsense frustrate or, even better, stop the mind (plus they are much more fun), which is advantageous when speaking of *this*.

Some passages are repetitive or say the same thing in different ways or by using different metaphors. This repetition is intentional because sometimes a point being repeated multiple times will cause something unnecessary to become dislodged, like a hammer repeatedly hitting a bent and useless nail.

—*Scott Moss*

THE CHAPTERS

This is everything,
and this is nothing.
Everything and nothing are one.
There is no possible name
that can be given to this oneness
other than, perhaps, *this*,
and even that falls completely short.

Out of this oneness
can spring the illusion
of twoness, the origin
of all suffering.

You can never escape
from the illusion of twoness,
not because it is not possible,
but because there is no you
to be able to escape.
You (the self) are twoness.

Liberation from twoness
happens as soon as the idea
falls away that there is
anything that can be liberated.

The eyes
and the light coming in
the eyes is the same thing.

The eyes are you.
The light is you.
The eyes are not you.
The light is not you.
There is no you
because you are already
everything and nothing,
or *this*, which is one.

The mind *despises* this,
because the mind wants
control and security that
springs forth as an
inevitable consequence of
the illusion of twoness.

The mind is this as well.
Nothing is not this
and therefore the mind
is not a problem, and of
course, there is no such
thing as the mind.

Liberation is like
that gleam on the highway.
It always disappears before you
get to it. The more you
speed up, the quicker
it disappears.

A student of Zen once
asked the master how
long it would take him
to become enlightened.
Ten years, said the master.
But what if I tried really
really hard, harder than everyone else?
Twenty years, said the master.

This story serves to clarify,
but even this story implies that
time is needed to reach
liberation, but time is nil.
It simply doesn't exist.
Time is an illusion of the self.
All there is is eternity,
which is not forever
and ever, but the absence
of time.

There are no failures
because all there is
is energy.

There are no successes
because all there is
is energy.

Matter can neither
be created nor destroyed.
Matter both exists
and doesn't exist
simultaneously.

Energy morphs.
All energy moves
towards unconstriction.
Unconstriction is also
known as unconditional
love, which can be
hidden or felt.

The self is the
perennial trickster,
inviting you through
the door, only to find
out once you get through
the door that you are on the
wrong side.

Then the self invites
you back through the door
to the right side again,
and you go through only
to find that you are once
again on the wrong side
of the door.

Then, maybe, it's seen
that there is no door
and nowhere needed to
get to.

There is no art,
but art happens.
And then it disappears
back into emptiness.

There is no politics,
but politics happens.
And then it drops
back into the unmanifested.

There is no nature
but nature happens.
And then it falls
back into nothingness.

There is no void,
but the void doesn't happen.
And then it vanishes
back into the void.

You will either recognize this
or not recognize this.
It is more accurate
to say that there will
either be a recognition or no
recognition. In order for it to
be recognized, the self must
disappear.

When it is recognized, there
is no way to communicate
what this is like through words,
although it can be hinted at.

The virtue of our charity quiets our will and causes us to wish for only what we have and thirst for nothing more. If we desired to be more exalted, our desire would be discordant with the will of the One who assigns us to this place, and you will see that this cannot hold in these circles, since love here is guaranteed, if you consider well the nature of these spheres. It is the essence of the blessed state that we keep ourselves within the divine desire so that our desires themselves may be unified.

—Dante, *Paradiso*

And again I say unto you, it is easier for a camel to go through the eye of a needle, than for a rich man to enter into the kingdom of God.

—Matthew 19-24

As long as you are proud you cannot know God. A proud man is always looking down on things and people: and, of course, as long as you are looking down you cannot see something that is above you.

—C.S. Lewis

All pain is a
constriction of energy.
All suffering is pain
viewed through the
filter of a self. The self
is an optical illusion
of consciousness,
so all suffering is
illusory, though it
doesn't feel like it.

Due to the brain being
able to apparently
create the illusion of
twoness (aka a self),
much of human
experience is suffering,
or at least that's the
way it seems to be.

The only thing real
is unconditional love,
or this.

Saying whatever happens happens
or saying nothing matters
is often spoken with sadness,
resignation, or despair.

Spoken from the space
of no self, these words are
pure liberation.

To be able to say these
things with a sense of
wonder means a different
perception has come in.

Liberation is pure wonder,
peace, joy (there are not
adequate words),
but for the self it is
the most catastrophic event
that can happen:
it is the death of the self.

What are hands for?

The typical answers:
Hands are for picking things up.
Hands are for carrying something
from one place to another.
And that's about it.

Even more important:
Hands are for letting things go.
Without being able to let things go,
hands would be useless.

This is not a religion.
Turning this into a
religion is like dissecting
a frog:
you must kill it first.
If this is about anything,
it is about life.

This is not a belief system.
In a religion, the tighter
you grasp the beliefs, the
more religious you are. With
this, the less you believe, the
closer this is.

This is not a prescription
for behavior. Being good
is not better than being
despicable in terms of this.
The light can fall upon
anything at any time.

That which emerges
from a place of no self
meets no
resistance from the world.

That which creates no
opposition springs from
nowhere and nothing.

That which emerges
from a place of self
meets
resistance from the world.

That which creates
opposition springs from
constriction and strain.

Nothing real can be threatened.
Nothing unreal exists.
Herein lies the peace of God.
—A Course in Miracles

Organizing this is not possible
because this is one. How can you
organize one?

The mind, in a seeming act of
rebellion against simplicity, which is
intolerable to the mind, will move to
make sense of this through
splitting it up into parts, but now
the frog dissection begins once
again.

But the mind is not an enemy.
It is just the mind, which is, of
course, oneness being the mind.

A good surfer
does not try to alter
the direction
of the waves.

A good seamstress
can alternate
between the current
stitch and a vision of
the finished garment.

An archer who cares
about hitting the bullseye
may hit the bullseye
but the shot is
inherently corrupt.

"The perfectest communication is heard of none."
—Emily Dickinson

This is best communicated
through parable, paradox,
or nonsense and humor.

This can be hinted at
or talked around,
but how could you
describe this using words?

Using words to describe
this is like making a
mosaic of a face
with only a few dozen tiles,
but words are some of the
only tools to communicate
the uncommunicateable.

This can be glimpsed
though words, but
silence is the greatest
communicator,
despite all these ridiculous
words written here.

Energy without an outlet
builds up pressure. Once the
pressure is overwhelming,
it erupts.

States of stress,
anxiety, and depression
are a building up of
pressure from an acute
sense of self. The more
acute the sense of self,
the greater the pressure.

Under enormous stress,
sometimes energy, in an
apparent act of mercy,
will reformulate in order
to relieve the burden.

This can be physical death
or a death while the body
still lives, called many things
such as liberation,
enlightenment, etc.

You cannot grasp
the truth, not because
the truth doesn't exist,
but because there is no
you to grasp it.

And, of course,
there is no such thing as
the truth.

All there is are words
on a page, and eyes
reading them.

All words that try
to communicate
infinity and eternity
fall short and are
quickly forgotten.
Well, usually.

All words that point
to this may ring true
for an instant or for
a few moments, and
then you quickly go
back to wanting
a new Porsche.

The self is like
quicksand that
fills itself back in as soon
as an opening is made.

When there is no self,
there is pure emptiness.

Everyone has had the experience
of laughing uncontrollably,
and then a reconstriction of
energy when the laughter
is winding down. You don't
want it to end, almost like an
anodyne wearing off.

When this emerges, it is like
being completely calm
and excited simultaneously,
a total peace
and harmony takes over.

Nothing matters,
and whatever happens happens.
Even death itself is a trifle
because things are seen for
exactly what they are, or
rather, this is seen for exactly
what this is.

No amount of
rearranging of outside
circumstances can
bring about inner-
peace and harmony.

Ask any dictator this.
They will not be honest
about it, or, more accurately,
they will not have enough
awareness because of their
desire to control things,
but ask them anyway.

Unless they'll kill you
for asking. Then don't ask.

Chuang Tzu was dreaming that he was a butterfly, flitting and flying about with no memory whatsoever of being Chuang Tzu. He woke up from the dream and he was, indeed, Chuang Tzu again, back in his own body. But now he couldn't tell if he had been Chuang Tzu dreaming that he was a butterfly, or if he was now a butterfly dreaming that he is Chuang Tzu. There must be some difference!

Irony, humor, and satirizing
those who claim to know all
give great pleasure.

People love meeting people
who make no pretense of knowing
because they recognize themselves
in the unknowingness.

Being able to laugh at
fragility and helplessness
is a massive source
of relief and unconstriction.

Those who sit with arms
crossed in light of humor
are prone to disease
and will likely die younger,
which just means the
return is more pressing.

Life thrives on flexibility.
Death embraces rigidity.

As we wade further
and further out into
the wide world,
there is always the
desire to return home,

home apparently being
lost forever.

But recapturing home
or pursuing the illusion
of it keeps up the misperception
that we are not home already,

and thus engenders
more suffering.

The more footprints
you make, the more the grass
repairs itself. There is nothing
that can be accomplished
that will not eventually
be undone.

Everything is undone
before it is done. Things
that are going to happen
have already happened.
Everything that has happened
and everything that can happen
and everything that will happen
is happening right now,
simultaneously.

This seems a good reason to do nothing.
Doing nothing might include
writing a book, opening a business,
having a family, or going to Tokyo
to order up some tasty ramen.

Doing nothing might also include sitting
and looking out the window for hours on end.

The more conservative you are
the more liberals you create.
The more liberal you are
the more conservatives you create.

Celebrating a conservative victory
is simultaneously celebrating
a liberal backlash.
Celebrating a liberal victory
is simultaneously celebrating
a conservative backlash.

The scale will tilt
back and forth in favor of
one side then the other,
but the fulcrum
remains forever fixed,
perfectly still.

The more stillness, the closer
this is. Stillness can be present
while in motion or while at rest.

Light can only emerge
from darkness.

The darker the source,
the brighter the light.

Light and darkness
are one.

This is infinite.
This is eternal.

This is an ultimate love
that has no opposite.

The mind will always
work to depose here and now
to bring about there and then
in an attempt to control,
evaluate, or gain position.
The mind can be looking
to either the past or the future.
The mind can never be
here and now.

There is nothing wrong with that.
There is nothing right with that.
That is the mind
doing what the mind does.
It is Being being the mind.
Resistance of the mind
strengthens the mind.
Nonresistance of the mind
strengthens the mind.

Connecting with your path
or, more insidiously,
connecting deeply with
your path, is simply another
way to keep the story of me alive.
There is no path
from here to here.

While you are connecting
deeply with your path,
a cat is sleeping in an askew
rectangle of sunlight.
A bicycle is riding by
outside in the light rain.
A breath is being taken.

The most subversive act
is nonresistance.
Those who seek out
opposition lose all power
when unopposed. This
does not mean that you
don't dodge a punch.

Fighting darkness
expands the darkness.

Whatever light falls upon
will brighten and become
light itself.

All concepts
will be overturned
because they are
like building blocks
that get rearranged
once a new block
is found. The human
brain is so limited
that it can never
understand everything,
although sometimes it
can glimpse this out of
the blue.

The human brain
is like a filter through
which this flows,
but it cannot ever fully
filter all that is,
like how a tiny funnel will
spillover when too much
is poured into it. The brain
is the tiniest of funnels,
yet cosmic in its scope.

To learn which questions are unanswerable,
and not to answer them: this skill is most
needful in times of stress and darkness.
—Ursula K. Le Guin

What is this hammer for?
A sensible question.
To drive nails.
To hit things that would
hurt your hand if you were
to use your hand.

What is this life for?
Now you have prescribed
the function of the mind
onto questions where it
has no business.

Asking these types of questions
in territory that is not the mind's
is like a mosquito trying to get
blood from a bronze bull.

Life is its own purpose.

When you have worn out
a set of clothes and throw
them away, do you feel
as if you have been diminished?

When the body wears out
and is thrown away,
will you feel as if you have
been diminished?

The body is simply like
a set of clothes that will
be thrown out when it
is old or damaged
beyond repair.

Essence endures. Essence is
incorruptible, eternal.

Seeing that nothing lasts,
you can resign yourself
to ultimate despair,

or you can go get
some roller skates
to ride around on.

What lasts is nothing,
and this nothing gives
birth to all of this
seemingly real
manifested world.

All there is is nothing.

Out of this nothing springs everything.
But this everything is also no thing.

This nothing allows eyes to see,
ears to hear, etc.

This nothing is home.
Everpresent, omnipotent yet
uncontrolling, and it doesn't
exist, nor does it have a will.
It is unconditional love.

When you drink coffee,
that is nothing tasting nothing,
and yet there is a cup of coffee there,
or maybe a cappuccino if
you're really into coffee.

*The cradle rocks above an abyss, and common sense
tells us that our existence is but a brief crack of light
between two eternities of darkness.*
—Vladimir Nabokov

*There are more things in heaven and earth,
Horatio, than are dreamt of in our philosophy.*
—Hamlet

*Once I could play what I heard inside me,
that's when I was born.*
—Charlie Parker

Mesmerized and hypnotized
by things in the manifested world,
the mystery is constantly
hidden outside of awareness.

Only when the manifested world
is looked past or seen through
can the mystery be glimpsed.

That which is worthwhile
does not need to be promoted.
That which needs to be promoted
is not worthwhile.

What is most fitting
falls into place without effort.
What is forced into place
is always under threat of
being dislodged.

The snow falls, each flake
exactly in its place.
Spring comes, and the
grass grows all by itself.

This message is
catastrophic to the self.
The self will resist this
with all of its might
because what the self
wants more than anything
is the story of me.

The self would rather
be miserable than
not exist, and it will
defend itself until the
last breath.

But, of course, there
never was a self, it was
simply the illusion
of twoness. When it's over,
there is unconditional love,
the single greatest threat
to the self.

This is a mystery, but
this is not a mystery
that can be solved.
If it could be solved,
it would not be this.

Abundance is the curse
of prosperity.
Satisfied desire is the misfortune
of desire.

The greater the indulgence in
a sought-out pleasure, the more
acute the corresponding pain.

Pleasure and pain
are the same thing.
Seeking out pleasure
at the exclusion of all pain
engenders more pain.
Seeking out pain
at the exclusion of pleasure
and you're a bit loony.

Joy, peace, and love emerge
from beyond the realm of
sensory pleasures.

Not knowing that you are grooming
and protecting a persona is a lack
of awareness. Awareness is
perfection. A lack of awareness
is also perfection. There is no
state that is better than any other
because all there is is oneness.

All personas fade or are cut down.
The more militant the persona,
the more likely it will be cut down
when a critical mass is reached.
Despite a persona's ability to
create followers and thereby
strengthen itself, it will blow up
like a balloon and then be either
slowly deflated or popped.

The desperation to protect a
persona comes out of the ignorance
that you think you are separate
from everything else.

To those of past
generations who never
tried to accomplish
anything big or
earth-shattering:

Thank you.

There is not less confusion
or anxiety by knowing more.

When nothing is known
and nothing is assumed
and nothing is guessed at,
clarity emerges.

Knowledge is an attempt
to gain a feeling of security.
This is not to say that some
knowledge doesn't serve a
purpose, like knowing how to
read a map or knowing how to
follow a recipe.

We can describe the laws
of gravity, for example,
sometimes ad nauseam,
but we can never truly
know what gravity is,
or why gravity is.

Even asking the question
of why gravity is gravity
shows the futility of all
apparent knowing.

Why do flowers open
when the sun comes out?
Because they open
when the sun comes out.

Penicillin and being able
to heat up rooms is remarkable,
but it is not the be-all and end-all.

Clinging to the self, to
what seems to be born and
what seems to have a
temporary continuance,
there is no peace.

Dying before the body
dies, there is only wonder.

Nobody can choose
to die before the body dies.
Nobody can choose to
surrender to what is.

When what seems to be born
and what seems to have a
temporary continuance dies,
all that's left is life.

Life in this form seems
to be lived by a separate
person, but this is the
illusion of the self.

Self-interest is friction.
Selflessness is harmony.

With no self present,
things flow effortlessly.

You cannot extinguish the self
because you are the self.

The self may or may not
fall away, but it has nothing
to do with you.

Upon physical death of
the body (the heart stops beating,
the brain stops working),
the self (that never actually
existed) is snuffed
out, and all that is left
is oneness, unconditional love,
this.

In the greatest artist
there is an element
of athleticism.

In the greatest athlete
there is an element
of artistry.

Energy manifests.
The type of energy
will determine the
style of manifestation.

Nobody is in control
of the type of energy
that is manifested.

Energy manifested that
is judged to be inferior
or superior is not worse or
better than any other
energy.

All is energy.
All is perfection.

Advocate peace,
bring about war.
Advocate war,
bring about peace.

Whatever is fought for
brings about its opposite.

When nothing is
advocated, things
simply happen
effortlessly.

Mind finds chalk
and a chalkboard
and writes H2O and O2.

Being sits on cliff's edge
looking out at ocean and sky,
breathing silently.

When I heard the learn'd astronomer,
When the proofs, the figures, were ranged in columns before me,
When I was shown the charts and diagrams,
to add, divide, and measure them,
When I sitting heard the astronomer where he lectured
with much applause in the lecture-room,
How soon unaccountable I became tired and sick,
Till rising and gliding out I wander'd off by myself,
In the mystical moist night-air, and from time to time,
Look'd up in perfect silence at the stars.
—Walt Whitman

Trying to find this
is like looking for
your sunglasses when
they are
on top of your head.

As light falls equally
and without exceptions
on those who we think
of as sinners and those
who we think of as saints,

thus this embraces
all there is, all that is
manifest, without
hesitation or prejudice,
without conditions,
unequivocally,
without any conception
of better or worse.

This is so omnipresent,
it is more often than not
missed, as fish do not
know what water is.

The self swims
against the current
or tries to redirect
the current.

The no self is
the current and
that which the
current changes.

This is a message with
no hope whatsoever.
This is a message with
no despair whatsoever.

Hope is positivity while
thinking about the self.
Despair is negativity while
thinking about the self.

This has nothing to do
with the self. The self
is the core illusion.

All there is is oneness.

Those who are active attest
that the active life is the best
life.

Those who are contemplative
speak about how being
contemplative is the best
life.

Is it a coincidence that we say
that the best is what we are
personally? Is it a coincidence
that people born in a certain
country think that it is the best
country in the world?

The ego (the self, the me)
is like a business strategist,
full of thoughts of ownership,
full of craftiness, full of
concerns about what's best
for this little bag of skin
and nothing else.

The fresher the water
the less we taste.
The purer the air
the less we smell.
The truer the sound
the less we hear.
The stiller the mind
the shorter is eternity.

The mind will either be
still or it will not be still.
You cannot still the mind
to experience this.
It is as futile as a hand
trying to pick itself up.

Letting the world take
you over is
letting yourself take
you over.

Taking control of yourself
is letting the world
take you over.

The world is already you,
and, of course, there is
no you.

You cannot be everything,
which is exactly what you are.

In its widest possible sense...a man's Self
is the sum total of all that he can call his,
not only his body and his psychic powers,
but his clothes and his house, his wife and children,
his ancestors and friends, his reputation and his works,
his lands and horses, and yacht and bank account.
All these things give him the same emotions.
If they wax and prosper, he feels triumphant;
if they dwindle and die away, he feels cast down.
—William James

The true value of a human being is determined primarily
by the measure and the sense in which he has
attained liberation from the self.
—Albert Einstein

When I state myself, as the representative of the verse,
it does not mean me, but a supposed person.
—Emily Dickinson

All desire is the desire
to return to this
original oneness
that is sensed on some
level by all though usually
resisted or repressed.

All seeking of gain,
advantage, and pleasure
is in fact an attempt to
distract the self from
the feeling of being
separate from oneness,

which it doesn't recognize
and in fact exacerbates
the feeling
of separation.

All eventually dissolves
save love.

Changing the world
is like moving sand around
on the beach:

The world will eventually
wipe clean all your
efforts, leaving no trace.

The self takes ownership
of its efforts, and takes
credit for what it perceives as
having done itself. Nobody
has ever done anything.

You have never done anything:
you are being lived.

This is infinite.
The further you
enter into it,
the more expansive
it becomes.

Upon the emergence of a
sense of self, oneness splits
asunder into a world that
can only be perceived in terms
of gain and loss,
advantage and disadvantage,
pleasure and pain,
etc.

Before the world ever
came into existence,
this is.

What did you look like
before your parents met?

Whoosh!

Talking about this
feels dead and tiresome.
It is like trying to
explain why a joke
is funny. You either
laugh or
you don't get it.

If you get it by talking
about it or having it
explained, there is
something unspontaneous
about it.

This will emerge
or it will not.
Either way,
it doesn't matter because
this is all there is.

The self is like
a squatter in the soul,
using every legal
means at its disposal
not to be evicted.

Comparing yourself to others
leads to a sort of misery
because you may see others
as having a better this or a
better that. Comparison,
of course, doesn't make any
sense in light of oneness.

It is like workers in a field
who are offered a wage, accept it,
and then become angry when
others arrive later and get
paid the same wage for
less work. Comparison
drains vital energy.

Nothing is better
or worse than anything
else, a statement that
is intolerable to the mind
which judges everything
as a comparison.

The mind is the industrious
organizer and categorizer,
judging all things as better
or worse in order to gain
advantage within the illusory
pleasure and pain viewpoint.

You are the ocean,
but you like to imagine
that you are a wave that has
formed and is not
connected to the ocean.

The apparent madness
and storminess that life in
a human body sometimes
feels like is actually
the perfect stillness
of the ocean as a whole.

Speaking about this
is somewhat futile
because there is

nothing to find,
nothing to understand,
nothing to solve,
nowhere to get to,
nobody home.

There are no teachers,
no seekers,
no paths,
no gurus,
no destinations.

Viewing the world
through the lens of
right and wrong is
a form of violence.

When two gorillas
square off and beat their
chests, they are both saying
"I'm right, you're wrong."

This world is an illusion.
The only thing real is spirit.*
This world is spirit.

*Substitute for *spirit* any word that makes sense here.
Some options are God, Tao, the everlasting,
Brahman, Allah, Snoopy, etc.

There is no way to jolt,
cajole, or practice your way
into is because this is all there is.

The mind lives in past
and future so that it can
chew on problems, thinking
in this way that it can move
towards is.

Completely engrossed in this,
it would be nearly impossible to
function in this world.

Completely cut off from this,
and one becomes lost in this world
as in a dark forest.

Sometimes the illusion
of twoness is so deeply
rooted that any mention
of oneness will be met
with confusion, ridicule,
or even anger.

Oneness is incredibly
threatening to a self
that wishes to remain
in a state of twoness out
of fear and insecurity.

Liberation is the single
greatest catastrophe to
the separate, seeking,
efforting self.

What we fear the most
and long for the most
is our own absence.

There is no escape
from the self because
any attempt to escape
from the self would be
the self itself trying
to free itself from the
self. It is like a tack
that doesn't exist
trying to remove itself
from the wall.

All there is is holding
a book in the hand, and
reading words on paper.

There is nothing new under the sun.
—Ecclesiastes

My mother sent for one of those squat, plump little cakes called "petites madeleines," which look as though they had been moulded in the fluted valve of a scallop shell. And soon, mechanically, dispirited after a dreary day with the prospect of a depressing morrow, I raised to my lips a spoonful of the tea in which I had soaked a morsel of the cake. No sooner had the warm liquid mixed with the crumbs touched my palate than a shudder ran through me and I stopped, intent upon the extraordinary thing that was happening to me. An exquisite pleasure had invaded my senses, something isolated, detached, with no suggestion of its origin. And at once the vicissitudes of life had become indifferent to me, its disasters innocuous, its brevity illusory—this new sensation having had on me the effect which love has of filling me with a precious essence; or rather this essence was not in me, it was me. I had ceased now to feel mediocre, contingent, mortal. Whence could it have come to me, this all-powerful joy? I sensed that it was connected with the taste of the tea and the cake, but that it infinitely transcended those savours, could, no, indeed, be of the same nature. Whence did it come? What did it mean? How could I seize and apprehend it? —Marcel Proust

Wherever you point the camera,
make sure to look closely at what the light is doing
before deciding to take the shot.
—Rolleiflex instruction manual

Imagine that the whole world
sees in black and white. One
morning, you wake up and you
see the world in color. How
can you communicate this to
others? A radical new perception.
Would anyone believe you?

Those who have awakened to
what might be called cosmic
consciousness have tried to
communicate it, and they have
often been met with ridicule,
shunning, or even violence.

This is the dilemma of trying to
communicate this. But those who
do communicate this are bringing
a message of pure salvation, the
relief of being nobody.

Within everyone, there is a
pilot light. This message may
reach the pilot light, and may
make someone light up with
the wonder of oneness.

And it may not. Either way,
it doesn't matter, because already
all is one, and all is perfection.

There is no such thing
as yesterday's light.

There is no such thing
as tomorrow's light.

All there is is
the ineffable
presence of
unconditional love.

Made in United States
Troutdale, OR
01/29/2024